ALL ABOUT
WHEELS
AND AXLES

Erinn Banting

LIGHTB◆X
openlightbox.com

LIGHTBOX

Go to
www.openlightbox.com
and enter this book's
unique code.

ACCESS CODE

L B R 3 4 7 7 3

Lightbox is an all-inclusive digital solution for the teaching and learning of curriculum topics in an original, groundbreaking way. Lightbox is based on National Curriculum Standards.

STANDARD FEATURES OF LIGHTBOX

 AUDIO High-quality narration using text-to-speech system

 ACTIVITIES Printable PDFs that can be emailed and graded

SLIDESHOWS Pictorial overviews of key concepts

VIDEOS Embedded high-definition video clips

 WEBLINKS Curated links to external, child-safe resources

TRANSPARENCIES Step-by-step layering of maps, diagrams, charts, and timelines

 INTERACTIVE MAPS Interactive maps and aerial satellite imagery

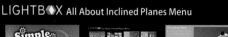

 QUIZZES Ten multiple choice questions that are automatically graded and emailed for teacher assessment

 KEY WORDS Matching key concepts to their definitions

CONTENTS

The Wheel and Axle

A wheel is a circle-shaped object that rotates, or turns, around its center. Often, the hub, or center, of a wheel is connected to a rod called an axle. The wheel and axle turn together around the same **axis**. Wheels and axles were first used thousands of years ago. Now, they help a wide range of tools and machines to operate. Vehicles such as cars and amusement park rides such as Ferris wheels are just some of the many devices that rely on wheels and axles.

The wheel and axle is a type of simple machine. A machine is a device that uses power to do a task. There are six kinds of simple machines. They are the inclined plane, the lever, the pulley, the screw, the wedge, and the wheel and axle. Simple machines make **work** easier, but they do not add **energy** of their own. Instead, simple machines change the **effort** needed to perform tasks.

3635–3370 BC
The oldest picture of a vehicle with wheels and axles is the flat stick figure of a cart found on a vase in Poland.

The screwdriver is a wheel and axle. This tool was invented in the **1400s**.

The largest rolling pin, which is a long wheel and axle, can be found on the roof of a bakery in **Victoria, Australia**.

Spokes connect the hub of a bicycle wheel to the round rim that supports the tire.

Simple Machines

The inclined plane and the lever are the most basic of all simple machines. They can even be found in other types of simple machines.

Types of Inclined Planes

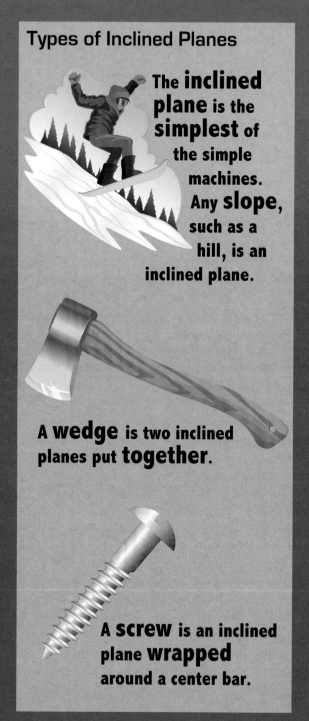

The **inclined plane** is the **simplest** of the simple machines. Any **slope**, such as a hill, is an inclined plane.

A **wedge** is two inclined planes put **together**.

A **screw** is an inclined plane **wrapped** around a center bar.

Types of Levers

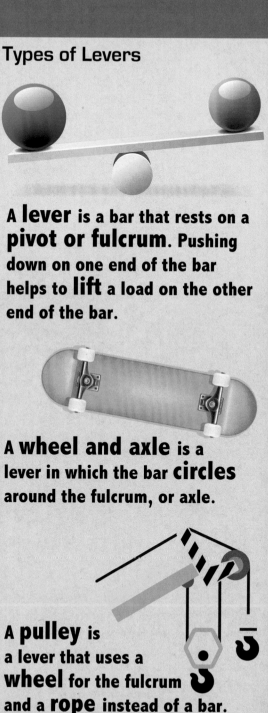

A **lever** is a bar that rests on a **pivot or fulcrum**. Pushing down on one end of the bar helps to **lift** a load on the other end of the bar.

A **wheel and axle** is a lever in which the bar **circles** around the fulcrum, or axle.

A **pulley** is a lever that uses a **wheel** for the fulcrum and a **rope** instead of a bar.

From Simple to Complex

Simple machines can be combined to make other kinds of machines. When simple machines are combined, the new device is often called a compound or complex machine. Wheels and axles are needed in many complex machines because they can transfer energy.

Drivetrain

A drivetrain is the group of parts that delivers power from a car's engine to spin one of the vehicle's axles. Many drivetrains include pulleys.

Cable Cars

Aerial cable cars use both pulleys and wheels and axles to move the carriages up a mountainside.

Jet Engine

Wheel-and-axle fans draw air into a jet engine. The engine mixes the air with fuel, burns the mixture, and sends burning gas out the back. This thrusts, or pushes, the plane forward.

Using Wheels and Axles

Gears on axles help produce power in many machines. A gear is a wheel with teeth on its edge. The teeth fit with teeth on another gear. When one gear turns, it makes the other one turn as well. In this way, **motion** transfers from the first gear to the second one.

The power and speed of turning gears can be changed for different needs. Large gears turn easily. However, they need to be turned quickly to push an object forward. More power has to be applied to turn smaller gears, but they can move an object faster.

Factory workers make very large gears for use in wind turbines, which produce electricity.

Wheels and Axles at Work

People all across the world use wheels and axles to make their work easier.

Cars and Trucks

Most land vehicles need wheels and axles to move. The engine makes power to turn the axles. That turns the wheels and moves the vehicle across the ground.

Watches

In some watches, a coiled spring unwinds and transfers power to a series of gears. The turning gears move the hands on the watch.

Trains

On many trains, an axle connects one wheel on each side of a train car to other wheels on the same side. Moving the first wheel turns the other wheels as well.

Computer Disks

An axle holds the disk in place inside a computer or DVD player. The axle spins the disk so the machine can read it.

Wheels and Axles of the World

Wheels and axles have many everyday uses. For example, a doorknob is a wheel that turns on an axle. An egg beater and many other kinds of small tools contain wheels and axles.

2 **GREAT BRITAIN** The Laxey Wheel near Ramsey on the Isle of Man is the largest working water wheel. Flowing water turns the wheel, making an axle spin. The axle has been used to power pumps that removed water from mine shafts.

1 **UNITED STATES** The largest paddle-wheel riverboat, the *American Queen*, is based in New Orleans, Louisiana. Its steam engine turns axles that spin paddle wheels, pushing the boat forward.

NORTH AMERICA

ATLANTIC OCEAN

SOUTH AMERICA

PACIFIC OCEAN

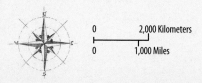

0   2,000 Kilometers

0   1,000 Miles

However, wheels and axles are also found in very large pieces of equipment. These devices are often used in industry and in transportation. They are found in theme parks. This map shows places where wheels and axles have big roles in large objects.

3

GERMANY The world's largest mining machines are bucket wheel excavators. Their huge wheels are mainly used to dig out coal at mines such as the one in Welzow, Germany.

ARCTIC OCEAN

ASIA

EUROPE

PACIFIC OCEAN

4

UNITED ARAB EMIRATES The world's largest Ferris wheel is being built on Bluewaters Island in Dubai. Called the Dubai Eye, the wheel will be 688 feet (210 meters) tall.

AFRICA

INDIAN OCEAN

AUSTRALIA

Ancient Wheels and Axles

The first forms of transportation did not have axles or wheels. This made moving people or **loads** from place to place difficult. Goods or building materials had to be carried or dragged along the ground. Dragging heavy objects involved a great deal of work. When wheels were invented, moving objects from one place to another became much easier.

Even before wheels were invented, early humans realized that rounded objects moved with greater ease. They made rollers by placing logs on the ground side by side. They laid materials on top of the logs to transport them. When the load was pulled, the logs rolled, and the load moved forward. According to some scientists, the shift from rollers to wooden wheels may have happened around 8000 BC.

❋ The first vehicles were carts or wagons with solid wheels. In some parts of the world, such carts are still used today.

Wheels and Axles Timeline

2000 BC
Two-wheeled vehicles called chariots are used in the Middle East.

680 BC
Chariot racing is added to the ancient Greek Olympic Games.

50 BC
In ancient Rome, ruler Julius Caesar builds a racetrack for chariots.

AD 1000s
The spinning wheel, which uses wheels and axles to make thread from fibers, is invented in China.

1478
Italian artist and inventor Leonardo da Vinci designs a car-like vehicle.

1817
The bicycle is invented.

1903
Henry Ford starts the Ford Motor Company and soon begins to produce cars in large numbers.

1885
In Germany, Karl Benz invents the first automobile sold to people.

1971
U.S. astronauts drive the Lunar Roving Vehicle on the Moon.

2010
The number of cars in the world passes 1 billion.

⚙ A person standing at the center of a hula hoop is the hoop's axis. He or she must move ankles, knees, and hips to create the forces that spin a hula hoop and keep it out of equilibrium.

Force and Movement

Force is a push or a pull that causes an object to move or change its direction. When an object is not moving, all of the forces pushing or pulling it are in balance. This balance is called equilibrium.

When scientists study how objects move, there are three important measurements they take into account. They figure out an object's weight, how fast it is moving, and the amount of force that is causing the object to move. Understanding forces, how forces affect objects, and how objects affect each other can make it easier to move objects.

Friction and Gravity

Friction is a force that occurs when two surfaces come in contact, such as when a box is pushed along the ground. Friction creates a gripping action that affects how much work is needed to move an object. When friction is greater, more work is needed. Round objects such as wheels create less friction than many other shapes because only a small part of a wheel touches the ground at any one time. This lack of friction is a main reason why using wheels can help people move heavy objects with less work.

Another force affecting how much work is needed to move an object is **gravity**. Earth's gravity pulls down on objects. This makes them harder to move.

Mass vs. Weight

Mass is how much material an object contains. Weight is how strongly gravity pulls on an object. An object's mass affects its weight. A rock has more mass than a marshmallow the same size, so the rock weighs more on Earth. However, mass and weight are not the same.

Mass is often measured in kilograms. A person with a mass of 91 kilograms weighs 200 pounds on Earth. This is because Earth's gravity pulls on a 91-kilogram mass with a force of 200 pounds. The Moon has much weaker gravity, so the same person weighs less there. The Moon's gravity pulls on a 91-kilogram mass with a force of only 33 pounds. That same person has almost no weight on a spacecraft because there is little gravity. He or she weighs about 0 pounds, even though the person's mass is still 91 kilograms.

Working with Force

In science, work happens when a force is used to move an object over a distance. For work to happen, the force must be applied in the same direction the object is moving. Lifting a rock off the ground is work because the force applied to pull the rock up is going in the same upward direction that the rock is moving.

Work also happens when a person pushes a rock forward along the ground. However, pushing against a very heavy rock and failing to move it is not work. The person may feel tired from his or her effort. Yet, if the rock has not moved, no work has taken place.

It can feel harder to pull a load than to push it. However, the amount of work is the same. The difference in how hard the task feels is related to the kinds of strain placed on the body's muscles.

As the force needed to move an object increases, the work involved in moving it also increases. This also applies to distance. The amount of work needed to move the object increases as the distance the object must move increases.

Simple machines make doing work easier. They do this by changing the amount and the direction of the force needed to move an object. Although less force is needed, simple machines require moving a greater distance.

Doing Work

In general, the amount of work performed equals the force used times the distance over which the force is applied. Distance is often measured in meters (m). Force is usually measured by a standard called the newton (N). Work is often measured by a standard called the joule (J). One joule equals one newton of force applied to move an object one meter.

A person pushes an object 5 meters with a force of 10 newtons.
The work is equal to 50 joules.

5 m x 10 N = 50 J

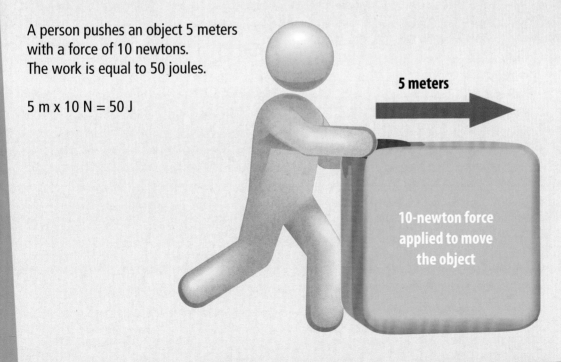

5 meters

10-newton force applied to move the object

On many tractors, the large back wheels power the vehicle's movement.

How Wheels and Axles Work

The wheel and axle makes work easier because it offers a **mechanical advantage**. As the wheel turns, the axle turns too. In many wheel-and-axle machines, the mechanical advantage is created because the axle spins with greater force than the larger wheel attached to it. The turning wheel and axle act as a lever that moves in a complete circle.

The greater the distance a wheel travels to complete one turn, the more force it transfers to the axle. In other words, as the size of the wheel increases, the force transferred to the axle increases as well. As with all simple machines, there is a trade-off between distance and force. A larger wheel transfers more force to its axle, but a larger wheel must travel a greater distance with each turn.

Calculating Effort

To determine the mechanical advantage of a wheel and axle, divide the **radius** of the wheel by the radius of the axle. The radius of this wheel is 24 inches (60 centimeters). The radius of this axle is 2 inches (5 cm). When 24 is divided by 2, the result is 12 (60 divided by 5 is 12). This means the force used to turn the wheel will be multiplied 12 times on the axle.

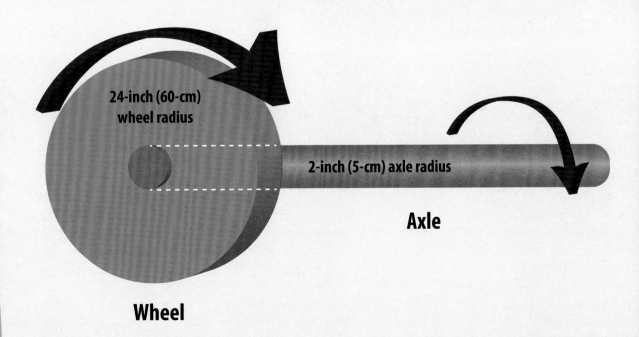

24-inch (60-cm) wheel radius

2-inch (5-cm) axle radius

Axle

Wheel

What Is a Mechanical Engineer?

Mechanical **engineers** design a variety of devices, from roller coasters to robots. These devices include machines used in industries, as well as machines that make people's lives easier and more enjoyable. Mechanical engineers study math and science in college, and they often earn advanced degrees. Mechanical engineers need creative skills in order to solve problems and invent tools. They must enjoy working with others because their projects can be large and complex.

Leslie Livesay

Leslie Livesay is a NASA engineer. As a child, Livesay learned that the *Voyager* spacecraft had passed the planet Saturn. She became interested in space, and she studied math and engineering. After college, she helped design the Mars *Pathfinder* rover. That vehicle was sent to Mars to study its surface. She has also worked to find planets outside Earth's solar system.

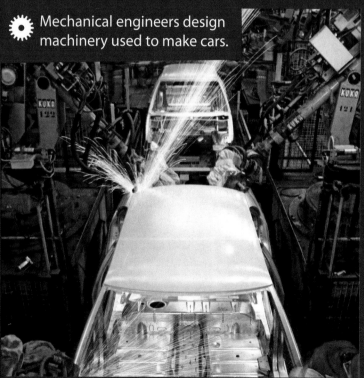

Mechanical engineers design machinery used to make cars.

Brain Teasers

1 What is a wheel?

2 What is an axle?

3 How many types of simple machines are there?

4 What is a gear?

5 What powers the gears in some watches?

6 What is a force?

7 When did Henry Ford start the Ford Motor Company?

8 What is friction?

9 What is mass?

10 How is work defined?

ANSWERS: 1. A wheel is a circle-shaped object that rotates around its center. **2.** An axle is a rod connected to the center of a wheel. **3.** There are six types of simple machines. **4.** A gear is a wheel with teeth around the edge. **5.** A coiled spring powers the gears in some watches. **6.** A force is a push or pull that causes an object to move or change direction. **7.** The year was 1903. **8.** Friction is a force created when two surfaces come in contact. **9.** Mass is how much material an object contains. **10.** Work is force applied over distance to move an object.

Wheels and Axles in Action

Learn more about motion by building a simple machine.

Materials Needed

two blank CDs or DVDs

marker

Directions

1 With the help of an adult, find two blank CDs.

2 Find a marker that fits into the holes in the center of the CDs.

3 Place the CDs on either end of the marker. You may need to remove the cap from the marker for the CD to fit.

4 Roll your new axle and wheels across a surface.

Key Words

axis: an imaginary line around which something turns

effort: the power being used to move something

energy: the power needed to do work

engineers: people who use science to solve practical problems

gravity: a force that pulls objects toward one another

loads: the objects or substances being worked on by a simple machine

mechanical advantage: a measure of how much easier a task is made when a simple machine is used

motion: the act or process of moving

radius: the distance from the center to the outside edge of a circle

work: power applied over distance to move an object

Index

LIGHTB◆X

➕ SUPPLEMENTARY RESOURCES

Click on the plus icon ➕ found in the bottom left corner of each spread to open additional teacher resources.

- Download and print the book's quizzes and activities
- Access curriculum correlations
- Explore additional web applications that enhance the Lightbox experience

LIGHTBOX DIGITAL TITLES
Packed full of integrated media

VIDEOS

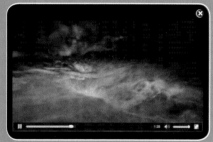

INTERACTIVE MAPS

WEBLINKS

SLIDESHOWS

QUIZZES

OPTIMIZED FOR

✓ **TABLETS**

✓ **WHITEBOARDS**

✓ **COMPUTERS**

✓ **AND MUCH MORE!**

Published by Smartbook Media Inc.
350 5ᵗʰ Avenue, 59ᵗʰ Floor
New York, NY 10118
Website: www.openlightbox.com

Library of Congress Control Number:
2016935461

ISBN 978-1-5105-0963-4 (hardcover)
ISBN 978-1-5105-0965-8 (multi-user eBook)

Printed in Brainerd, Minnesota, United States
1 2 3 4 5 6 7 8 9 0 20 19 18 17 16

032016
030916

Project Coordinator Heather Kissock
Art Director Terry Paulhus

Photo Credits
Every reasonable effort has been made to trace ownership and to obtain permission to reprint copyright material. The publisher would be pleased to have any errors or omissions brought to its attention so that they may be corrected in subsequent printings. The publisher acknowledges Getty Images, Corbis, and iStock as its primary image suppliers for this title.